SHAPING MATERIALS
IN MY MAKERSPACE

by Rebecca Sjonger

CRABTREE
PUBLISHING COMPANY
WWW.CRABTREEBOOKS.COM

Author:
Rebecca Sjonger

Series research and development:
Reagan Miller
Janine Deschenes

Editorial director:
Kathy Middleton

Editor:
Janine Deschenes

Proofreader:
Kelly Spence

Design, prepress, and photo research:
Katherine Berti

Print and production coordinator:
Katherine Berti

Photographs:
iStockphoto: front cover (boy)
p. 6, 7, 18 (bottom)
Steve Messam: p. 19 (top)
All other images by Shutterstock

Library and Archives Canada Cataloguing in Publication

Sjonger, Rebecca, author
       Shaping materials in my makerspace / Rebecca Sjonger.

(Matter and materials in my makerspace)
Includes index.
Issued in print and electronic formats.
ISBN 978-0-7787-4621-8 (hardcover).--
ISBN 978-0-7787-4627-0 (softcover).--
ISBN 978-1-4271-2051-9 (HTML)

       1. Materials--Juvenile literature. 2. Makerspaces--Juvenile literature.
I. Title.

TA403.2.S566 2018   j620.1'1   C2017-907640-X
                                                              C2017-907641-8

Library of Congress Cataloging-in-Publication Data

Names: Sjonger, Rebecca, author.
Title: Shaping materials in my makerspace / Rebecca Sjonger.
Description: New York, New York : Crabtree Publishing Company, [2018] |
   Series: Matter and materials in my makerspace | Includes index.
Identifiers: LCCN 2017057959 (print) | LCCN 2018005229 (ebook) |
   ISBN 9781427120519 (Electronic) |
   ISBN 9780778746218 (hardcover : alk. paper) |
   ISBN 9780778746270 (pbk. : alk. paper)
Subjects: LCSH: Materials--Properties--Juvenile literature. |
   Materials--Experiments--Juvenile literature. | Makerspaces--Juvenile literature.
Classification: LCC QC173.36 (ebook) | LCC QC173.36 .S5654 2018 (print) |
   DDC 620.1/1--dc23
LC record available at https://lccn.loc.gov/2017057959

Crabtree Publishing Company

www.crabtreebooks.com   1-800-387-7650

Printed in the U.S.A./032018/BG20180202

Published in Canada
Crabtree Publishing
616 Welland Ave.
St. Catharines, Ontario
L2M 5V6

Published in the United States
Crabtree Publishing
PMB 59051
350 Fifth Avenue, 59th Floor
New York, New York 10118

Published in the United Kingdom
Crabtree Publishing
Maritime House
Basin Road North, Hove
BN41 1WR

Published in Australia
Crabtree Publishing
3 Charles Street
Coburg North
VIC 3058

CONTENTS

YOU CAN BE A MAKER!

Makers learn by solving problems and creating new things. They use their imaginations to dream up new ways to do tasks or use objects. Anyone can be a maker! The ideas in this book will help you get started.

WORK WITH OTHER MAKERS

Makers share their skills and supplies with one another. They also team up to share their ideas. **Makerspaces** are places where makers work together. There could be one in your community. If not, you and your friends could set up your own makerspace.

No right or wrong!

Forget the rules and get ready to do things in a new way. Makers know:

- Your imagination is one of the most important tools you can use!
- Every idea could lead you in a new direction.
- Running into a problem is a chance to rethink your plans.

Makers learn by sharing their ideas for reaching a goal.

MATTER AND MATERIALS

You will shape **many** materials **as a maker.** They are all **made of** matter. **Matter is anything that takes up space and has** mass. **Mass is the amount of material in matter.**

WHERE DO MATERIALS COME FROM?

We find many materials in nature. Water and flowers are examples of natural materials. People make other materials, such as pencils and paper. Find out more about natural and human-made materials on pages 10–11.

DESCRIBING MATERIALS

Each material has **properties**. These are the ways we describe them. Strength, weight, **texture**, and **flexibility** are different properties of materials. Exploring properties helps makers sort materials and choose which materials work best for different purposes, or uses.

SOLIDS AND LIQUIDS

Materials can come in different forms, called **states**. The state of a material is one of its main properties. Two of the main states are **solids** and **liquids**. Solids keep their shape. They cannot be poured. Liquids can be poured. They flow into the shape of whatever holds them.

liquid

solid

solid

solid

BE A PROPERTY EXPLORER

Some properties are measured with tools. For example, you could use a ruler to find the length of a material. To find its weight, you could use a scale.

USE YOUR SENSES

Other properties can be sensed, or explored using your senses. Ask yourself questions as you explore materials with your senses. What does it feel like when you touch it? What does it look like? Could you taste, listen to, or smell it?

PROPERTY CHALLENGE

Each maker project needs materials with different properties. Some common properties and examples of materials are listed below. Explore them to help you get started:

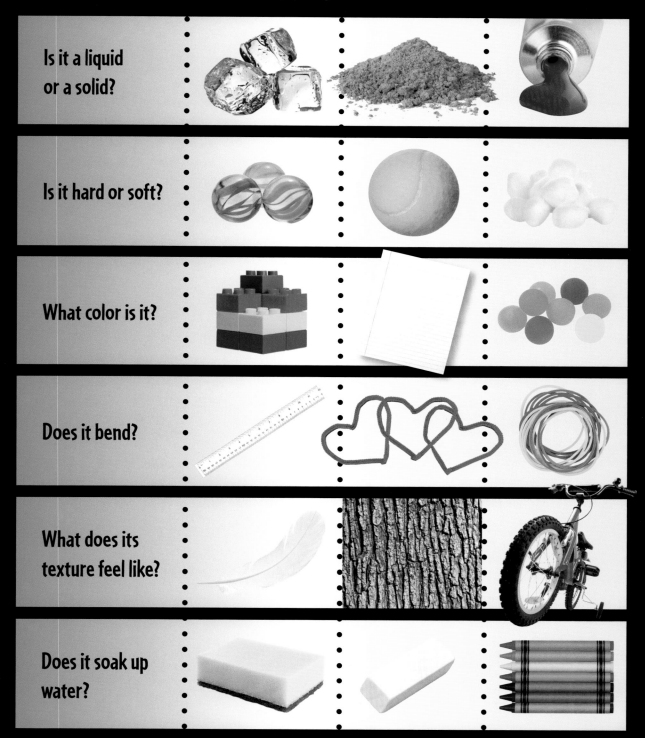

Is it a liquid or a solid?

Is it hard or soft?

What color is it?

Does it bend?

What does its texture feel like?

Does it soak up water?

NATURAL AND HUMAN-MADE

Go on a materials hunt! First, look for liquids and solids that are part of the natural world. Rocks, trees, and animals are all natural materials. Next, hunt for natural materials that humans shaped into a new object. For example, look for carvings that are made from wood.

What natural materials can you find in your community?

IDEAS FROM NATURE

Makers get more than materials from nature. They get ideas from it, too! You could make something cool with a piece of **driftwood** by looking at its color or shape. You could also look at how strong it is, or whether it floats. The properties of driftwood might give you ideas for how to shape materials to make a boat!

HUMAN-MADE MATERIALS

Makers also use human-made matter. Plastic is an example of a solid made by humans. It can be shaped in many ways. Look at a plastic cup or toy to explore some of its other properties. For example, plastic does not break apart easily. It does not soak up water. It also comes in many colors! These properties make it a common material.

MAKER TIPS

Looking at properties and materials is just one part of being a maker. Another big part is brainstorming at the start of each project. Come up with as many ideas as you can in just five minutes. Choose one idea to try first. Be sure to listen to everyone's ideas if you work with a team.

PLAN IT OUT

After you have chosen an idea, make a plan with steps you can follow. Sketch the parts of your creation. Measure your materials. Stay open to new ideas! Remember, your project might change along the way.

Step 1
Write down solids to use.

Step 2
Write down ways to shape solids.

Step 3
Choose a solid that is easy to shape.

Step 4
Choose two ways of shaping.

Step 5
Test ways of shaping.

Goal
Shape a solid in two different ways.

Try writing your ideas in a ladder. Write your goal at the top. Then, starting from the bottom, write down each of the steps you will take to reach your goal.

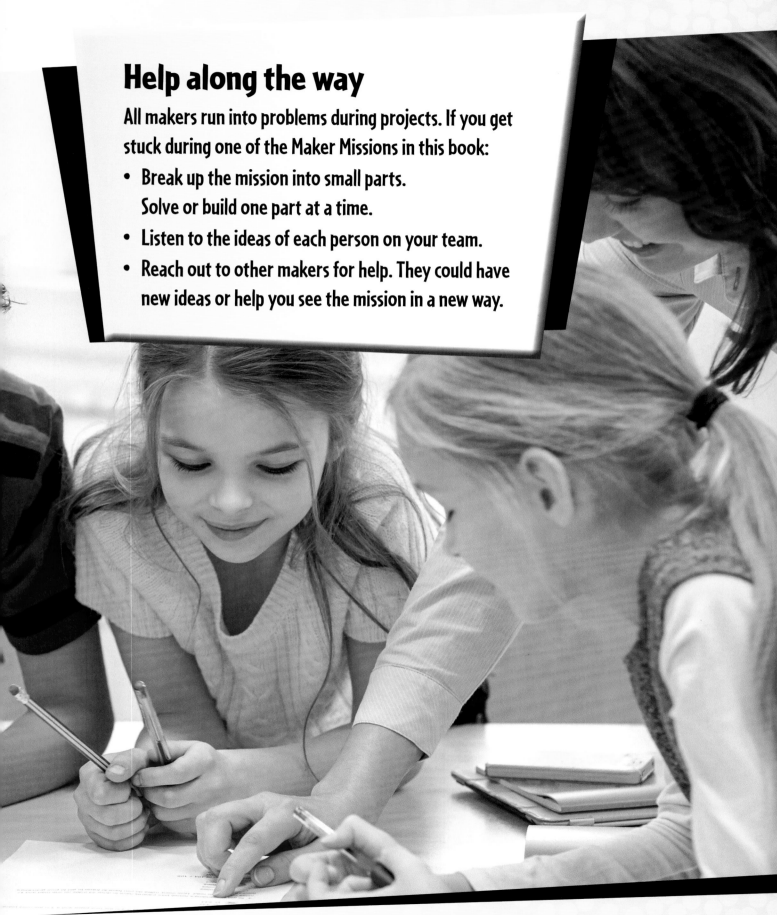

Help along the way

All makers run into problems during projects. If you get stuck during one of the Maker Missions in this book:

- Break up the mission into small parts.
  Solve or build one part at a time.
- Listen to the ideas of each person on your team.
- Reach out to other makers for help. They could have new ideas or help you see the mission in a new way.

METAL MATERIALS

Humans make metals from natural materials. Metals are solid materials that are usually hard and shiny. They come from solids found under the ground. Objects made of metal can last for a long time. People can bend or cut metal to shape it into many things. They can also melt metals into liquids, then shape them by drying them in molds. For simple projects, metals can also be attached together using tape, glue, or other joining materials.

Car parts and jewelry are two examples of shaped metals. Can you think of any others?

STRONG STRUCTURES

Wood and metal are common building materials. They have different properties and purposes. Compare them to see which one you would use to make a **structure**. Think about these questions:

- Which solid is stronger?
- Is one more likely to split or fall apart over time?
- Would wood or metal burn faster in a fire?

Metal is often the best choice for structures! It is strong, it lasts a long time, and it resists fire.

Try it!

To try shaping metal, check out the Maker Mission on the next page. Remember to start by planning!

MAKE A METAL STRUCTURE

Your mission is to make a strong metal structure. It must be at least 12 inches (30.5 cm) high. The base can be any size. It must be able to hold up your favorite T-shirt!

MAKER MISSION

Materials

- Paper
- Pencil
- Ruler
- Paper clips
- Metal wire
- Metal hangers
- Glue, tape
- T-shirt

MAKE IT SAFE

Be careful when you work with metal materials. They can be sharp! Ask an adult for help.

GLUE

THINK ABOUT IT

Materials → Which properties should you explore as you choose your materials?

How many ways could you change the shapes of your metal materials?

How could using different shapes be helpful?

Design

Where is a good spot to build your structure?

Do you think the size of the structure's base matters?

How will you connect the parts to make your structure?

How will you place the T-shirt over the frame?

MISSION ACCOMPLISHED

Was your metal structure strong enough to hold up a T-shirt? If it fell apart, don't give up! What could you do differently on your next try? Build on your success with a new project.

Check out Endless Ideas on page 30.

SHAPE FOR STRENGTH

Often, makers shape materials to create an object. The metal structure in the last challenge is an example of this. But they can also shape matter to change its properties!

PAPER PROPERTY CHANGE

See for yourself how shaping materials changes how strong they are. Follow these steps and notice how the strength of the paper changes.

1. Grab two sheets of paper.
2. Tear one sheet into two pieces. Note how much effort, or work, it took to do it.
3. Fold the second sheet in half.
4. Fold it in half again two more times.
5. Now, try tearing the folded paper. How much effort did it take?

Which sheet of paper was stronger? Shaping the second paper changed its strength!

Folding paper changes more than its strength. It also changes its size!

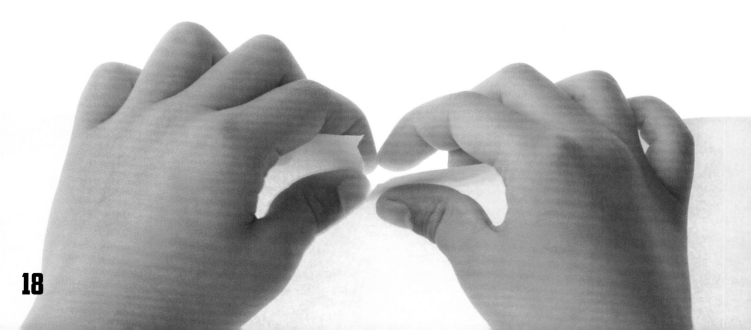

18

MANY WAYS OF SHAPING

Folding is one of many ways to make materials stronger. For example, you could stack them to build them up. You could also braid or twist solids. This changes their size and strength. How else could you strengthen materials?

Try it!

Brainstorm ways to shape materials to make them stronger. Then head to the next Maker Mission!

MAKE IT STRONGER

The next challenge is all about strength! Use at least two materials to make a strong cord. It must be at least 2 feet (61 cm) long. The cord should stay in one piece when its ends are pulled in opposite directions.

Materials

- Paper
- Pencil
- Tape measure
- Cotton materials, such as string or skipping ropes
- Plastic materials, such as trash bags or hosing
- Wrapping paper

THINK ABOUT IT

Design

Look back to pages 18–19. Which ways of shaping matter might work for this challenge?

Will the way you shape your materials shorten them? Does that change how much you need to start with?

Materials

What properties do you need to think about when choosing your materials?

Size

What do you need to measure?

Does it matter if your materials are different lengths?

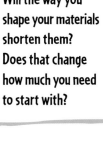

MISSION ACCOMPLISHED

Is your cord 2 feet (61 cm) or longer? Does it stay in one piece when its ends are pulled in opposite directions? If it needs to be stronger, should you change your materials or how you shaped them?

Flip to page 30 for ideas for what to do with your cord.

CHANGING TEMPERATURES

Changing the temperature of matter can change its state. What happens when you pour pancake batter into a hot pan? The heat changes the liquid into a tasty solid!

SHAPE-SHIFTER

The shape of a material changes when its state changes. Picture your pancake batter before and after you cook the pancakes. Can you think of more examples from your kitchen?

MELT AND HARDEN

When some solids get hot enough, they turn into a liquid. Have you ever left out a chocolate bar in hot weather? It may have become a liquid mess in the wrapper! Liquids turn into solids when they cool down. You could shape liquid chocolate by pouring it into a mold.

How does changing their temperature affect the states and shapes of these foods?

Try it!

Are you ready for a yummy maker challenge? Get started on the next page. This is a great project to do with a team of other makers!

MAKE A TREAT

Change the state of liquids and shape them into frozen treats. You must be able to see at least two separate layers of colors in them.

Materials

- Paper
- Pencil
- Molds, such as disposable cups, ice cube trays, or plastic muffin trays
- Two or more kinds of juice that are different colors
- Wooden craft sticks or large toothpicks
- Tape, elastics, string
- Freezer

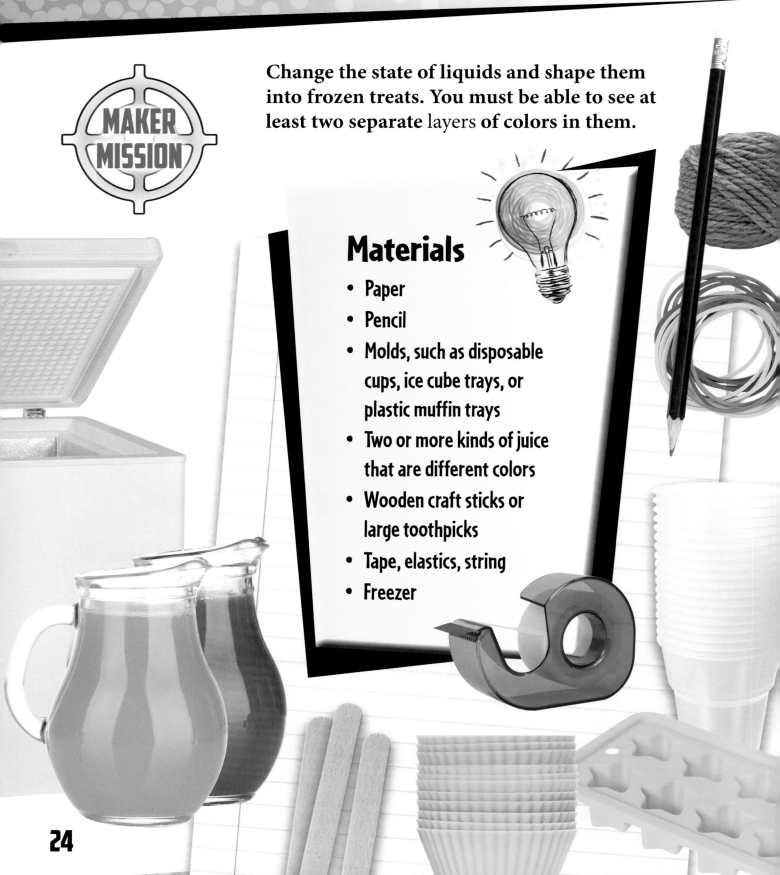

THINK ABOUT IT

Design → How will you keep the different colors of juice from mixing together?

How will you know when the new shape is formed?

Should you work in stages?

How will you get your treats out of the molds when they are ready?

Could you use water to heat the outside of the mold and loosen the frozen juice?

Size

How much room will you need in a freezer?

Materials

Which material would make a good handle?

What could you do to keep the handles from falling over in the liquid?

MISSION ACCOMPLISHED

Did you make a frozen treat with colorful layers? If you need help, go back to the Maker Tips on pages 12–13.

When your treats meet your goals, look at Endless Ideas on page 30.

SHAPE UP!

Makers shape materials in many ways. So far, you tested what happens when you add layers. You explored shaping with molds. You changed the temperature of materials. But there are even more shaping ideas to discover!

PROPERTY POWER

Think about the properties of a material before you shape it. Ask yourself questions. Is it hard or soft? Does it bend? Will it break easily? Knowing what you are working with will help get you started. Then fire up your imagination to see what you can make!

TOOL TIME

Tools can help you shape materials. Any solid with a hollow area, or empty space, in it could be a mold. Rollers are also useful for shaping solids, such as dough. Cookie cutters can make many shapes. Your fingers are some of the best tools for shaping materials!

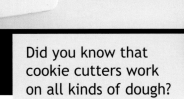

Did you know that cookie cutters work on all kinds of dough?

Artists shape materials in many different ways to make sculptures.

Try it!

Get ready to shape a solid in as many ways as you can. If you get stuck in the next challenge, try a new material or way of shaping.

MAKE MANY SHAPES

Make a sculpture by shaping a soft solid. Your goal is to shape the material that makes up your sculpture in at least five different ways.

Materials

- Paper
- Pencil
- Roller
- Cookie cutters
- Pasta or cookie press
- Dull knife, scissors
- Soft material that can be shaped, such as play dough or clay
- Work surface

MAKE IT SAFE

Always ask an adult for permission before using any sharp tools!

THINK ABOUT IT

Design

What will your sculpture look like? Will it be shaped like an object found in nature, such as an animal? Draw some ideas!

How will you put the five pieces together?

Materials

Is the temperature of your solid important in this challenge?

What are some ways you could use your hands to shape the material? For example, how could you make long strands or balls?

MISSION ACCOMPLISHED

Does your sculpture include at least five ways of shaping the solid? If not, look back through the book for more ideas to try.

Check out more challenges on the next page!

ENDLESS IDEAS

Go beyond the Maker Missions!
Give these ideas a try:

Make a metal structure

pages 16–17

- Keep going up! Can you double the height of your creation?
- Which other solids could you shape into a structure? For example, try using craft sticks, straws, or cardboard.

Make it stronger

pages 20–21

- Make a game of tug-of-war! Use your cord or make a longer one.
- Could you use your cord to lift or carry objects?

Make a treat

pages 24–25

- What other treats could you make with molds?
- Ask an adult to help you experiment with chocolate, Jell-O, or other foods.

Make many shapes

pages 28–29

- What would happen if you used the same tools with a different material?
- How would working with something new change how you shape it?

LEARNING MORE

BOOKS

Challoner, Jack, and Maggie Hewson. *Matter and Materials*. Kingfisher, 2013.

Rompella, Natalie. *Experiments in Material and Matter with Toys and Everyday Stuff*. Capstone Press, 2015.

Rustad, Martha. *What Is It Made Of?: Noticing Types of Materials*. Millbrook Press, 2016.

Thomas, Isabel. *Experiments with Materials*. Heinemann-Raintree, 2015.

WEBSITES

Check out a cool paper-shaping challenge:
http://pbskids.org/designsquad/parentseducators/resources/paper_table.html

Take shaping play dough to a whole new level:
www.sciencebuddies.org/science-fair-projects/references/squishy-circuits-recipes

Experiment with materials to shape strong structures:
www.scientificamerican.com/article/popsicle-stick-trusses-what-shape-is-strongest

GLOSSARY

base The lowest part of an object or structure that supports it, or keeps it upright

brainstorm To list many ideas—no matter how silly—as quickly as possible

driftwood Wood, such as tree branches, that float in water

flexibility Able to bend without breaking

layer Matter that covers a surface or lies above or beneath another

liquid Matter that can be poured and takes on the shape of its container

makerspace A place where makers work together and share their supplies and skills

mass The measurable amount of material in matter

material Any substance that matter is made up of

matter Any material that takes up space and has mass

molds A hollow container that shapes materials

property A characteristic that describes matter

scale A tool that measures an object's weight, or how heavy it is

solid Matter that does not flow and cannot be poured

state The form that matter takes, such as a solid or a liquid

structure An object that is built using solid materials

temperature The measure of how hot or cold something is

texture The look or feel of an object, such as soft or rough

INDEX

ABOUT THE AUTHOR

Rebecca Sjonger is the author of more than 50 children's books. She has written numerous titles for the *Be a Maker!* and the *Simple Machines in My Makerspace* series.